INTRODUCTION

M000098762

Sight words are the words most frequently used and repeated in books and written material. A sight vocabulary is a list of words a child knows by sight, without having to sound the words out. Knowing sight words helps build speed and fluency when reading, and increases reading comprehension. The words included in this book are basic words your child can learn to recognize just by looking at them.

Here's what's inside:

Look at the sight word. Say it aloud. Trace the gray letters, then write the word yourself!

a

A

When the word begins the sentence, it starts with a capital letter.

a

a

A

I have _____ red coat.

TRACE AND LEARN
SIGHT WORDS!

PETER PAUPER PRESS, INC.
White Plains, New York

PETER PAUPER PRESS

In 1928, at the age of twenty-two, Peter Beilenson began printing books on a small press in the basement of his parents' home in Larchmont, New York. Peter—and later, his wife, Edna—sought to create fine books that sold at "prices even a pauper could afford."

Today, still family owned and operated, Peter Pauper Press continues to honor our founders' legacy of quality, value, and fun for big kids and small kids alike.

Images used under license from Shutterstock.com

Designed by Margaret Rubiano

Copyright © 2019
Peter Pauper Press, Inc.
Manufactured for Peter Pauper Press, Inc.
202 Mamaroneck Avenue
White Plains, NY 10601 USA
All rights reserved
ISBN 978-1-4413-3114-4
Printed in China

Published in the United Kingdom and Europe by
Peter Pauper Press, Inc. c/o White Pebble International
Unit 2, Plot 11 Terminus Road
Chichester, West Sussex PO19 8TX, UK

7 6 5 4 3

Visit us at www.peterpauper.com

Look at the sight word. Say it aloud. Trace the gray letters, then write the word yourself!

about

About

When the word begins the sentence, it starts with a capital letter.

about

about

About

There are ten cows.

Look at the sight word. Say it aloud. Trace the gray letters, then write the word yourself!

after  After

When the word begins the sentence, it starts with a capital letter.

after

after

After

Summer comes

spring.

Look at the sight word. Say it aloud. Trace the gray letters, then write the word yourself!

all

All

When the word begins the sentence, it starts with a capital letter.

all

all

All

Let's _____ go to the beach.

Look at the sight word. Say it aloud. Trace the gray letters, then write the word yourself!

am

When the word begins the sentence, it starts with a capital letter.

am

am

Am

I _____ going to the fair.

Look at the sight word. Say it aloud. Trace the gray letters, then write the word yourself!

and

And

When the word begins the sentence, it starts with a capital letter.

and

and

And

Bob _____ Dan

are having a party.

Look at the sight word. Say it aloud. Trace the gray letters, then write the word yourself!

are

Are

When the word begins the sentence, it starts with a capital letter.

are

are

Are

They _____ having fun.

Look at the sight word. Say it aloud. Trace the gray letters, then write the word yourself!

as

As

When the word begins the sentence, it starts with a capital letter.

as

as

As

The unicorn is white _____ snow.

Look at the sight word. Say it aloud. Trace the gray letters, then write the word yourself!

at  At

When the word begins the sentence, it starts with a capital letter.

at

at

At

Let's go to the game _____ noon.

Look at the sight word. Say it aloud. Trace the gray letters, then write the word yourself!

ate

Ate

When the word begins the sentence, it starts with a capital letter.

ate

ate

Ate

Someone _____ all the desserts.

Look at the sight word. Say it aloud. Trace the gray letters, then write the word yourself!

away  Away

When the word begins the sentence, it starts with a capital letter.

away

away

Away

We're going next week!

Look at the sight word. Say it aloud. Trace the gray letters, then write the word yourself!

back

Back

When the word begins the sentence, it starts with a capital letter.

back

back

Back

I will be right
.

Look at the sight word. Say it aloud. Trace the gray letters, then write the word yourself!

ball

Ball

When the word begins the sentence, it starts with a capital letter.

ball

ball

Ball

Throw the
to me.

Look at the sight word. Say it aloud. Trace the gray letters, then write the word yourself!

be  Be

When the word begins the sentence, it starts with a capital letter.

be

be

Be

I will _____ at the park.

Look at the sight word. Say it aloud. Trace the gray letters, then write the word yourself!

been

Been

When the word begins the sentence, it starts with a capital letter.

been

been

Been

I have _____

reading.

Look at the sight word. Say it aloud. Trace the gray letters, then write the word yourself!

big

Big

When the word begins the sentence, it starts with a capital letter.

big

big

Big

What a dog!

Look at the sight word. Say it aloud. Trace the gray letters, then write the word yourself!

boy

Boy

When the word begins the sentence, it starts with a capital letter.

boy

boy

Boy

Adam is a

Look at the sight word. Say it aloud. Trace the gray letters, then write the word yourself!

but 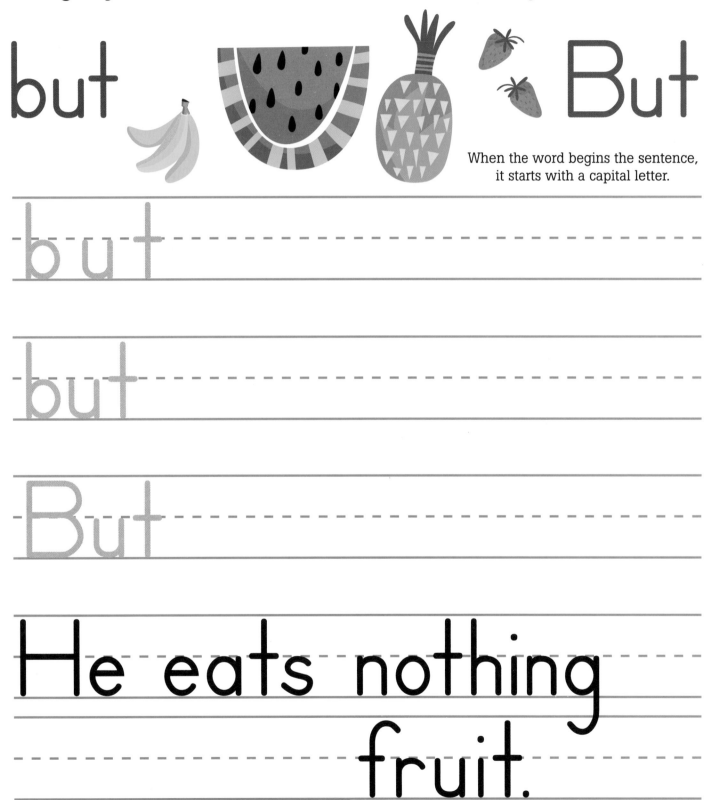 But

When the word begins the sentence, it starts with a capital letter.

but

but

But

He eats nothing fruit.

Look at the sight word. Say it aloud. Trace the gray letters, then write the word yourself!

by

By

When the word begins the sentence, it starts with a capital letter.

by

by

By

Come sit _____

me.

Look at the sight word. Say it aloud. Trace the gray letters, then write the word yourself!

came 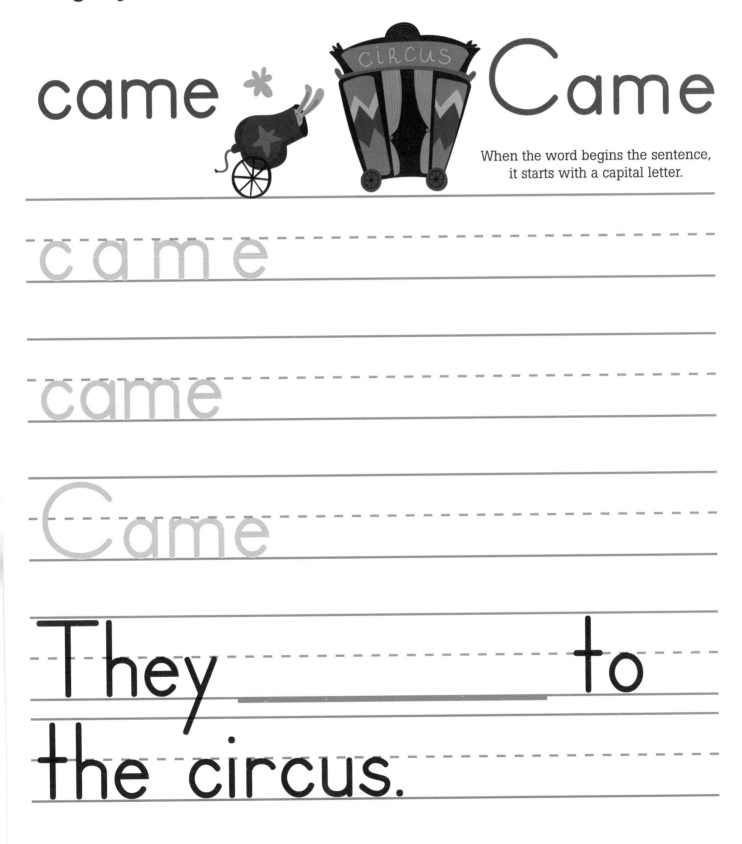 Came

When the word begins the sentence, it starts with a capital letter.

came

came

Came

They _____ to the circus.

Look at the sight word. Say it aloud. Trace the gray letters, then write the word yourself!

can

Can

When the word begins the sentence,
it starts with a capital letter.

can

can

Can

_____ you get the pencils?

Look at the sight word. Say it aloud. Trace the gray letters, then write the word yourself!

could  Could

When the word begins the sentence, it starts with a capital letter.

could

could

Could

_____ we have ice cream?

Look at the sight word. Say it aloud. Trace the gray letters, then write the word yourself!

day

Day

When the word begins the sentence, it starts with a capital letter.

day

day

Day

What _____ is it today?

Look at the sight word. Say it aloud. Trace the gray letters, then write the word yourself!

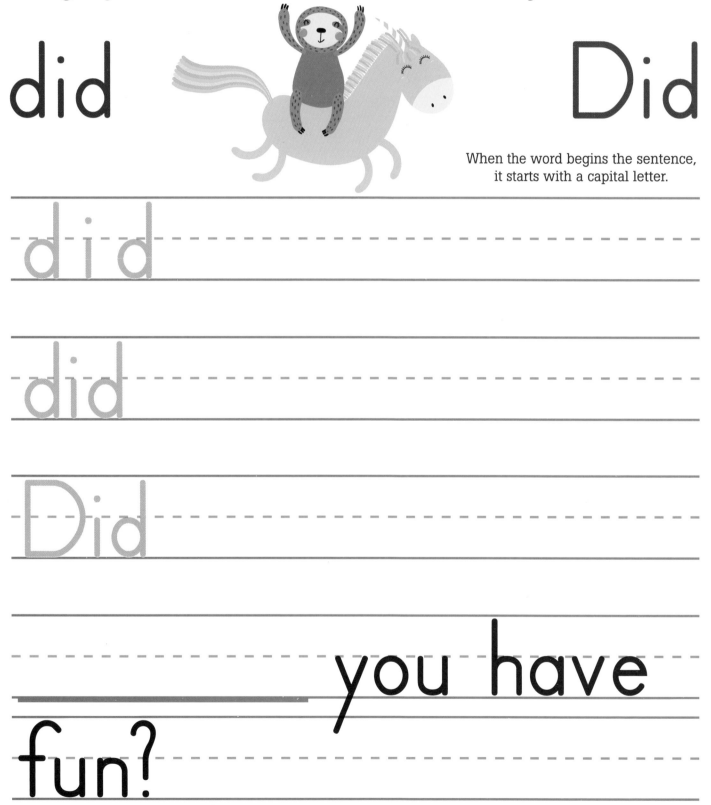

did

Did

When the word begins the sentence, it starts with a capital letter.

did

did

Did

_____ you have fun?

27

Look at the sight word. Say it aloud. Trace the gray letters, then write the word yourself!

do

Do

When the word begins the sentence, it starts with a capital letter.

do

do

Do

you want to go with me?

Look at the sight word. Say it aloud. Trace the gray letters, then write the word yourself!

down

Down

When the word begins the sentence, it starts with a capital letter.

down

down

Down

My pants won't fall .

Look at the sight word. Say it aloud. Trace the gray letters, then write the word yourself!

eat

Eat

When the word begins the sentence, it starts with a capital letter.

eat

eat

Eat

What do you want to ___?

Look at the sight word. Say it aloud. Trace the gray letters, then write the word yourself!

for

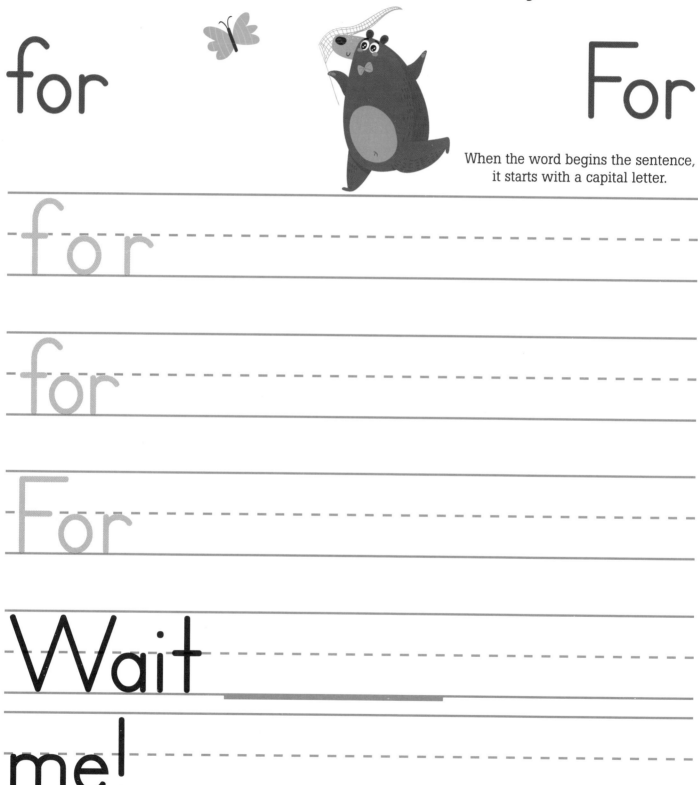

For

When the word begins the sentence, it starts with a capital letter.

for

for

For

Wait

me!

Look at the sight word. Say it aloud. Trace the gray letters, then write the word yourself!

from   From

When the word begins the sentence,
it starts with a capital letter.

from

from

From

I am _____

France.

Look at the sight word. Say it aloud. Trace the gray letters, then write the word yourself!

funny

Funny

When the word begins the sentence, it starts with a capital letter.

funny

funny

Funny

I'm being

.

Look at the sight word. Say it aloud. Trace the gray letters, then write the word yourself!

get

Get

When the word begins the sentence, it starts with a capital letter.

get

get

Get

Let's

going.

Look at the sight word. Say it aloud. Trace the gray letters, then write the word yourself!

girl

Girl

When the word begins the sentence, it starts with a capital letter.

girl

girl

Girl

The
is happy.

Look at the sight word. Say it aloud. Trace the gray letters, then write the word yourself!

go

Go

When the word begins the sentence,
it starts with a capital letter.

go

go

Go

We should _____

home.

Look at the sight word. Say it aloud. Trace the gray letters, then write the word yourself!

good

Good

When the word begins the sentence, it starts with a capital letter.

good

good

Good

That is _____

news!

Look at the sight word. Say it aloud. Trace the gray letters, then write the word yourself!

have 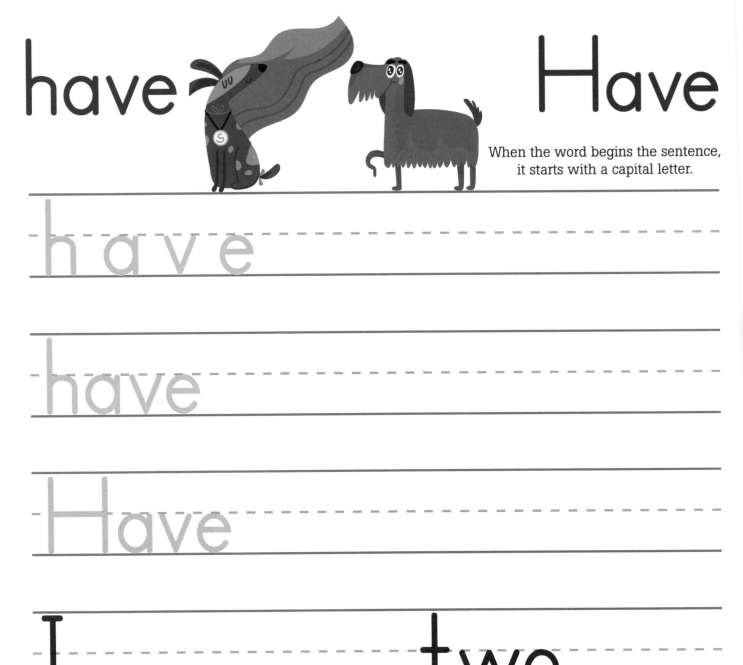 Have

When the word begins the sentence, it starts with a capital letter.

have

have

Have

I _____ two dogs.

Look at the sight word. Say it aloud. Trace the gray letters, then write the word yourself!

he

He

When the word begins the sentence, it starts with a capital letter.

he

he

He

_____ has a

cat.

Look at the sight word. Say it aloud. Trace the gray letters, then write the word yourself!

her

Her

When the word begins the sentence, it starts with a capital letter.

her

her

Her

She rode

horse.

Look at the sight word. Say it aloud. Trace the gray letters, then write the word yourself!

here  Here

When the word begins the sentence, it starts with a capital letter.

here

here

Here

_____ are some

coins.

Look at the sight word. Say it aloud. Trace the gray letters, then write the word yourself!

him

Him

When the word begins the sentence, it starts with a capital letter.

him

him

Him

I like _____

very much.

Look at the sight word. Say it aloud. Trace the gray letters, then write the word yourself!

I

I

The word I is always capitalized whether it begins a sentence or not.

I

I

I

_____ am going

swimming.

Look at the sight word. Say it aloud. Trace the gray letters, then write the word yourself!

in

In

When the word begins the sentence, it starts with a capital letter.

in

in

In

I'm _____ my warm bed.

Look at the sight word. Say it aloud. Trace the gray letters, then write the word yourself!

into

Into

When the word begins the sentence, it starts with a capital letter.

into

into

Into

Let's go the garden.

45

Look at the sight word. Say it aloud. Trace the gray letters, then write the word yourself!

is

Ada   Page   Jonah

Casey   Robin

Is

When the word begins the sentence, it starts with a capital letter.

is

is

Is

What _____ your name?

Look at the sight word. Say it aloud. Trace the gray letters, then write the word yourself!

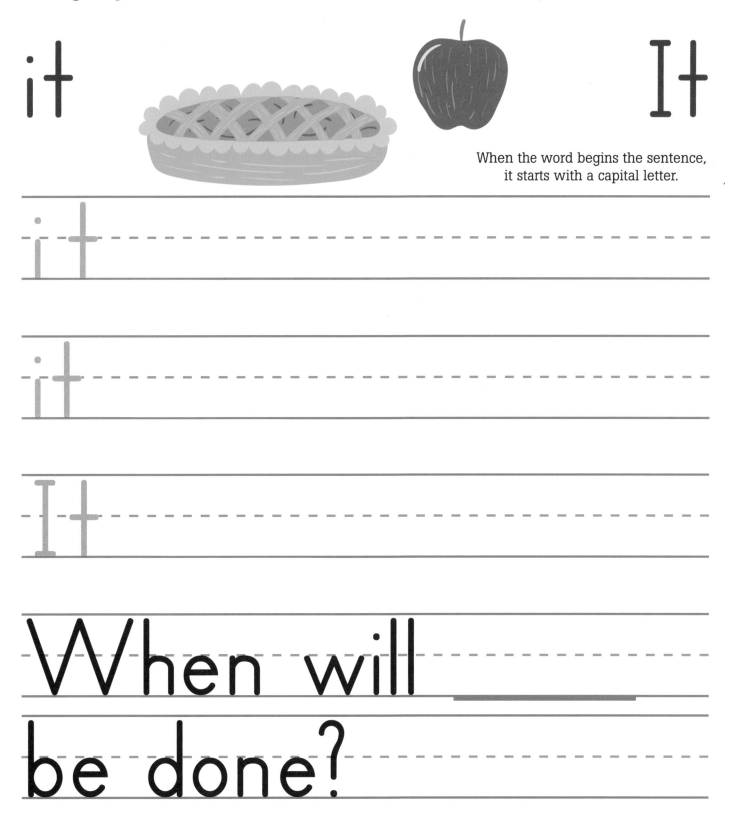

it

It

When the word begins the sentence, it starts with a capital letter.

it

it

It

When will _____ be done?

Look at the sight word. Say it aloud. Trace the gray letters, then write the word yourself!

like

Like

When the word begins the sentence, it starts with a capital letter.

like

like

Like

I _____ all cats.

Look at the sight word. Say it aloud. Trace the gray letters, then write the word yourself!

little   Little

When the word begins the sentence, it starts with a capital letter.

little

little

Little

An ant is very

_____ .

Look at the sight word. Say it aloud. Trace the gray letters, then write the word yourself!

long  Long

When the word begins the sentence, it starts with a capital letter.

long

long

Long

That dog has hair.

Look at the sight word. Say it aloud. Trace the gray letters, then write the word yourself!

look  Look

When the word begins the sentence, it starts with a capital letter.

look

look

Look

_____ at the

elephant!

Look at the sight word. Say it aloud. Trace the gray letters, then write the word yourself!

man  Man

When the word begins the sentence, it starts with a capital letter.

man

man

Man

A _____ is sleeping in a boat.

Look at the sight word. Say it aloud. Trace the gray letters, then write the word yourself!

me

Me

When the word begins the sentence, it starts with a capital letter.

me

me

Me

Do you want to go?

Look at the sight word. Say it aloud. Trace the gray letters, then write the word yourself!

must   Must

When the word begins the sentence, it starts with a capital letter.

must

must

Must

We _____ get some lunch.

Look at the sight word. Say it aloud. Trace the gray letters, then write the word yourself!

my

My

When the word begins the sentence, it starts with a capital letter.

my

my

My

Do you like shoes?

Look at the sight word. Say it aloud. Trace the gray letters, then write the word yourself!

new

New

When the word begins the sentence, it starts with a capital letter.

new

new

New

I have

green boots.

Look at the sight word. Say it aloud. Trace the gray letters, then write the word yourself!

no

No

When the word begins the sentence, it starts with a capital letter.

no

no

No

_____, I can't eat any more.

Look at the sight word. Say it aloud. Trace the gray letters, then write the word yourself!

not

Not

When the word begins the sentence, it starts with a capital letter.

not

not

Not

I'm _____ very sleepy.

58

Look at the sight word. Say it aloud. Trace the gray letters, then write the word yourself!

now  Now

When the word begins the sentence,
it starts with a capital letter.

n o w

now

Now

_____ let's have
some fun!

Look at the sight word. Say it aloud. Trace the gray letters, then write the word yourself!

of

Of

When the word begins the sentence, it starts with a capital letter.

of

of

Of

We ran out fuel.

Look at the sight word. Say it aloud. Trace the gray letters, then write the word yourself!

off   Off

When the word begins the sentence, it starts with a capital letter.

off

off

Off

Turn _____
the alarm clock.

Look at the sight word. Say it aloud. Trace the gray letters, then write the word yourself!

on

On

When the word begins the sentence, it starts with a capital letter.

on

on

On

Turn ____ the radio.

Look at the sight word. Say it aloud. Trace the gray letters, then write the word yourself!

one

One

When the word begins the sentence, it starts with a capital letter.

one

one

One

There is only cupcake left!

Look at the sight word. Say it aloud. Trace the gray letters, then write the word yourself!

our

Our

When the word begins the sentence, it starts with a capital letter.

our

our

Our

We are on way!

Look at the sight word. Say it aloud. Trace the gray letters, then write the word yourself!

out

Out

When the word begins the sentence, it starts with a capital letter.

out

out

Out

I'm going _____

now.

· ·

Look at the sight word. Say it aloud. Trace the gray letters, then write the word yourself!

over

When the word begins the sentence, it starts with a capital letter.

over

over

Over

The lemur flew our heads.

Look at the sight word. Say it aloud. Trace the gray letters, then write the word yourself!

play

Play

When the word begins the sentence, it starts with a capital letter.

play

play

Play

Let's _____

outside.

Look at the sight word. Say it aloud. Trace the gray letters, then write the word yourself!

please   Please

When the word begins the sentence, it starts with a capital letter.

please

please

Please

_____ come to

tea.

Look at the sight word. Say it aloud. Trace the gray letters, then write the word yourself!

put

Put

When the word begins the sentence,
it starts with a capital letter.

put

put

Put

_____ your shoes

here.

Look at the sight word. Say it aloud. Trace the gray letters, then write the word yourself!

read

Read

When the word begins the sentence, it starts with a capital letter.

read

read

Read

Let's _____ a book.

Look at the sight word. Say it aloud. Trace the gray letters, then write the word yourself!

ride

Ride

When the word begins the sentence, it starts with a capital letter.

ride

ride

Ride

Let's _____ on the llama.

Look at the sight word. Say it aloud. Trace the gray letters, then write the word yourself!

run

Run

When the word begins the sentence, it starts with a capital letter.

run

run

Run

I like to _____ as fast as I can!

Look at the sight word. Say it aloud. Trace the gray letters, then write the word yourself!

saw

Saw

When the word begins the sentence, it starts with a capital letter.

saw

saw

Saw

I _____ a hippo today.

Look at the sight word. Say it aloud. Trace the gray letters, then write the word yourself!

say **HELLO** Say

When the word begins the sentence,
it starts with a capital letter.

say

say

Say

Can you _____

hello?

74

Look at the sight word. Say it aloud. Trace the gray letters, then write the word yourself!

see

See

When the word begins the sentence, it starts with a capital letter.

see

see

See

Do you _____ the windmill?

Look at the sight word. Say it aloud. Trace the gray letters, then write the word yourself!

she

She

When the word begins the sentence, it starts with a capital letter.

she

she

She

_____ loves to

dance.

Look at the sight word. Say it aloud. Trace the gray letters, then write the word yourself!

sit

Sit

When the word begins the sentence, it starts with a capital letter.

sit

sit

Sit

Will you _____ down?

Look at the sight word. Say it aloud. Trace the gray letters, then write the word yourself!

so

So

When the word begins the sentence, it starts with a capital letter.

so

so

So

It is _____ bright!

Look at the sight word. Say it aloud. Trace the gray letters, then write the word yourself!

soon

Soon

When the word begins the sentence, it starts with a capital letter.

soon

soon

Soon

I will fall asleep.

Look at the sight word. Say it aloud. Trace the gray letters, then write the word yourself!

that

That

When the word begins the sentence, it starts with a capital letter.

that

that

That

_____ is a pink armadillo.

Look at the sight word. Say it aloud. Trace the gray letters, then write the word yourself!

the  The

When the word begins the sentence,
it starts with a capital letter.

the

the

The

_____ duck has

three babies.

Look at the sight word. Say it aloud. Trace the gray letters, then write the word yourself!

them 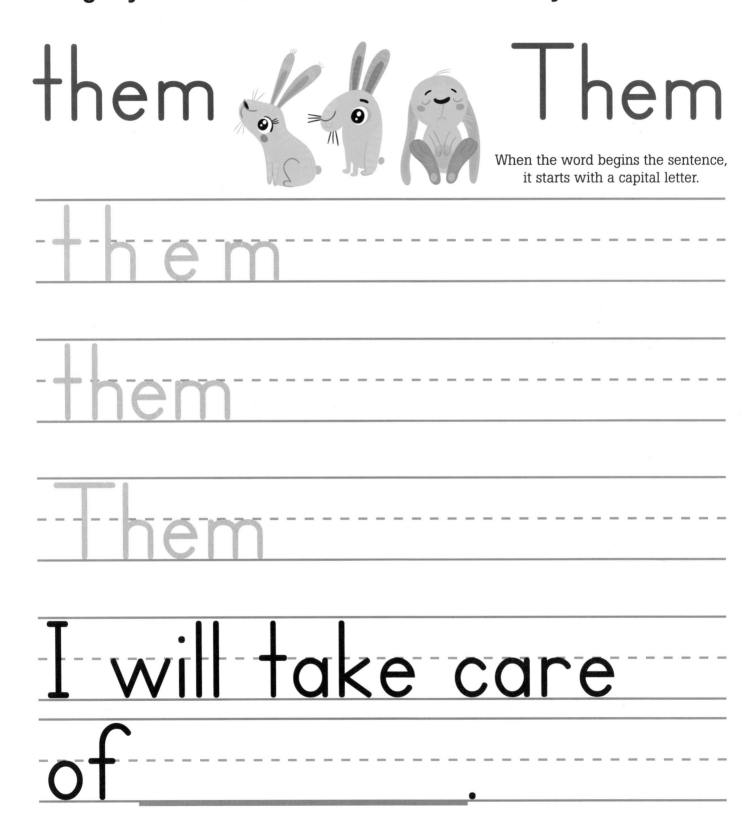 Them

When the word begins the sentence, it starts with a capital letter.

them

them

Them

I will take care of _____.

Look at the sight word. Say it aloud. Trace the gray letters, then write the word yourself!

there  There

When the word begins the sentence, it starts with a capital letter.

there

there

There

_____ is the

ship.

Look at the sight word. Say it aloud. Trace the gray letters, then write the word yourself!

they

They

When the word begins the sentence, it starts with a capital letter.

they

they

They

_____ are

green.

Look at the sight word. Say it aloud. Trace the gray letters, then write the word yourself!

this

This

When the word begins the sentence, it starts with a capital letter.

this

this

This

_____ is

yummy.

Look at the sight word. Say it aloud. Trace the gray letters, then write the word yourself!

to

To

When the word begins the sentence, it starts with a capital letter.

to

to

To

Can we go _____
the party?

Look at the sight word. Say it aloud. Trace the gray letters, then write the word yourself!

too

Too

When the word begins the sentence,
it starts with a capital letter.

too

too

Too

I am _____

busy.

Look at the sight word. Say it aloud. Trace the gray letters, then write the word yourself!

under  Under

When the word begins the sentence, it starts with a capital letter.

under

under

Under

He lives
the ground.

Look at the sight word. Say it aloud. Trace the gray letters, then write the word yourself!

up

Up

When the word begins the sentence, it starts with a capital letter.

up

up

Up

Look _____ in the sky!

Look at the sight word. Say it aloud. Trace the gray letters, then write the word yourself!

us

Us

When the word begins the sentence, it starts with a capital letter.

u s

us

Us

Tell _____ which way to go.

Look at the sight word. Say it aloud. Trace the gray letters, then write the word yourself!

very  Very

When the word begins the sentence, it starts with a capital letter.

very

very

Very

I love you much.

Look at the sight word. Say it aloud. Trace the gray letters, then write the word yourself!

want 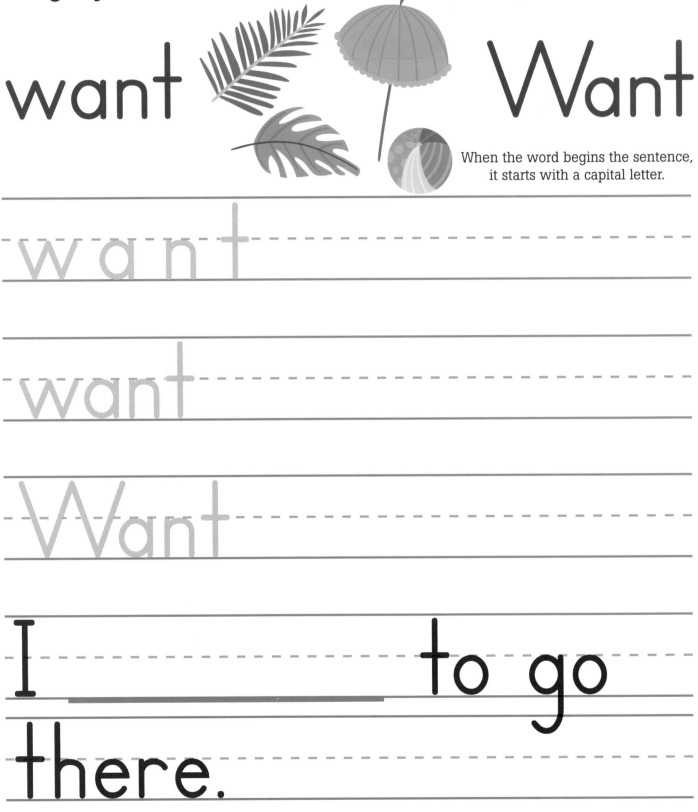 Want

When the word begins the sentence, it starts with a capital letter.

want

want

Want

I _____ to go there.

Look at the sight word. Say it aloud. Trace the gray letters, then write the word yourself!

was

Was

When the word begins the sentence, it starts with a capital letter.

was

was

Was

I _____ hanging up the birdhouse.

Look at the sight word. Say it aloud. Trace the gray letters, then write the word yourself!

we

We

When the word begins the sentence, it starts with a capital letter.

we

we

We

_____ are having a party.

Look at the sight word. Say it aloud. Trace the gray letters, then write the word yourself!

well

Well

When the word begins the sentence, it starts with a capital letter.

well

well

Well

I don't feel

.

Look at the sight word. Say it aloud. Trace the gray letters, then write the word yourself!

went

Went

When the word begins the sentence, it starts with a capital letter.

went

went

Went

I _____ to the parade.

Look at the sight word. Say it aloud. Trace the gray letters, then write the word yourself!

what

What

When the word begins the sentence, it starts with a capital letter.

what

what

What

_____ time

is it?

Look at the sight word. Say it aloud. Trace the gray letters, then write the word yourself!

where 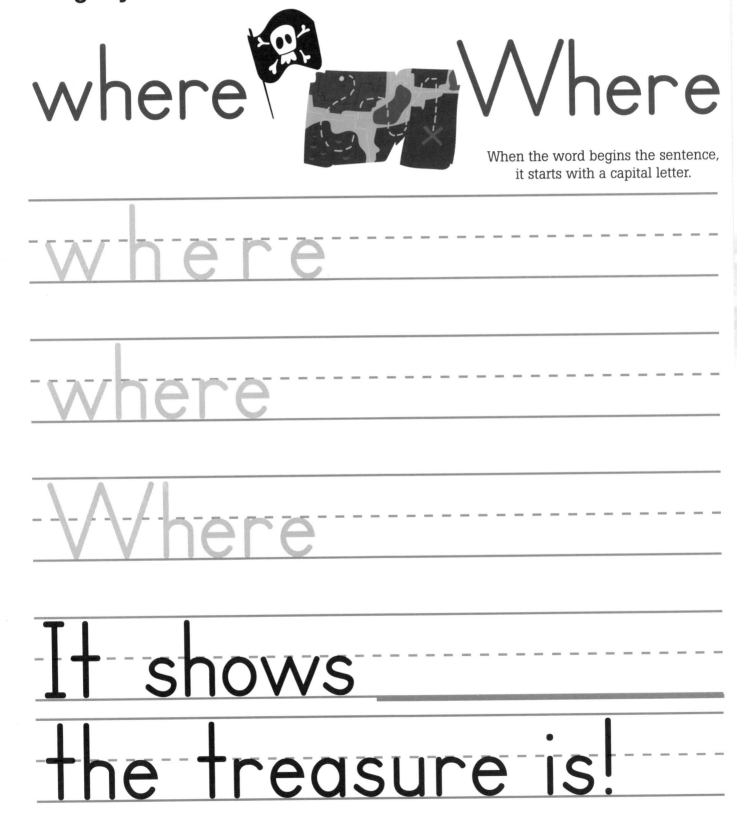 Where

When the word begins the sentence, it starts with a capital letter.

where

where

Where

It shows the treasure is!

Look at the sight word. Say it aloud. Trace the gray letters, then write the word yourself!

who  Who

When the word begins the sentence, it starts with a capital letter.

who

who

Who

_____ are you going with?

Look at the sight word. Say it aloud. Trace the gray letters, then write the word yourself!

will

Will

When the word begins the sentence, it starts with a capital letter.

will

will

Will

I _____ paint you a picture.

Look at the sight word. Say it aloud. Trace the gray letters, then write the word yourself!

with  With

When the word begins the sentence, it starts with a capital letter.

with

with

With

Play music

us!

Look at the sight word. Say it aloud. Trace the gray letters, then write the word yourself!

yes  Yes

When the word begins the sentence, it starts with a capital letter.

y e s

yes

Yes

_____, I would love some ice cream.

Look at the sight word. Say it aloud. Trace the gray letters, then write the word yourself!

you

When the word begins the sentence, it starts with a capital letter.

you

you

You

I will see _____

again soon.

Word Search

The words in each puzzle grid are hidden vertically, horizontally, backward, or diagonally. Words can overlap but they are always found in a straight line without skipping over any letters. Your job is to find and circle them, crossing them off the word list as you go along.

t	m	f	d	g	e	e	n
n	n	a	j	l	i	s	u
e	y	i	t	n	y	b	o
w	w	t	c	u	a	z	y
o	i	a	r	i	n	e	j
l	m	b	m	i	a	u	t
e	n	o	o	s	m	o	a
m	q	a	e	w	n	k	a

big	day	man	soon
came	little	not	went

Write the sight word

there

There

Find and circle the same word below

we	top	they	went
the	she	see	there
me	there	bet	can
can	that	been	we
it	we	there	put

Now read the word

- There is going to be a party later.
- Let's go over there.
- We don't know how to get there.
- There isn't much to tell.

Look at the sight words below. Find and circle each of these words in the following sentences.

came   not   funny   long   into

- The cartoon was funny.

- Class lasted a long time.

- I'm not going to the show.

- Let's go into my house.

- She came to class late.

Write the sight word

from

From

Find and circle the same word below

who	can	eat	from
the	from	him	by
fun	he	bet	from
for	them	here	we
it	from	are	like

Now read the word

- He leapt from his horse.
- Is the ranch far from here?
- She pushed the idea from her mind.
- The flower grew from a seed.

Sight Word Scramble

Unscramble the sight words	Practice writing each word

onos

ader

tawh

amce

oogd

albl

goln

good   soon   long   read   what   came   ball

Write the sight word

please

Please

Find and circle the same word below

please	must	they	please
little	on	new	the
man	our	please	now
what	please	was	with
well	over	went	please

Now read the word

- Please don't get up.
- Will you please help me?
- Turn off the light, please.
- Please tell me.

Look at the sight words below. Find and circle each of these words in the following sentences.

over   ride   play   must   out

- Can you jump over the puddle?

- Please put out the fire.

- May I ride the horse?

- Let's play in the sandbox!

- Must we go to sleep?

Sight Word Scramble

Unscramble the sight words

Practice writing each word

hatt

aypl

enw

voer

rea

neeb

mthe

new   been   play   them   over   are   that

Word Search

The words in each puzzle grid are hidden vertically, horizontally, backward, or diagonally. Words can overlap but they are always found in a straight line without skipping over any letters. Your job is to find and circle them, crossing them off the word list as you go along.

b	t	e	j	y	m	d	p
e	t	u	b	i	a	l	q
e	d	f	i	n	a	w	b
n	g	i	b	y	w	a	a
a	b	o	u	t	l	e	k
p	z	e	a	l	g	y	v
e	f	c	h	e	o	g	d
d	a	y	s	b	k	k	n

about	ball	big	day
away	been	boy	play